Kdrama Fan Journal

드라마 팬 저널

© Marie Cole, 2020. All rights reserved. This book or any portion thereof may not be reproduced or used in any manner whatsoever without the express written permission of the author.

Dear Fellow K-drama Fan,

I created this journal with my own habits in mind. Inside you'll find monthly questionnaires, fun k-drama inspired games, k-drama summary pages, k-drama Master Lists for your favorite streaming networks and a k-drama tracker!

I hope you love writing in journal as much as I do! If you have any feedback for features you'd like or ones you didn't feel free to email me at mariecolebooks@gmail.com

saranghaeyo!
-Marie

KDRAMA TRACKER
TITLE

Title	OPENED EYE KISS	HOLDING HANDS	KIMCHI SLAP	<3 2ND MALE LEAD	SHOWER SCENE	PLAYSET SWINGS	STALKING	WALL SLAM	FINGER HEART	OVERHEAD HEART			

KDRAMA TRACKER

TITLE

	OPENED EYE KISS	HOLDING HANDS	KIMCHI SLAP	<3 2ND MALE LEAD	SHOWER SCENE	PLAYSET SWINGS	STALKING	WALL SLAM	FINGER HEART	OVERHEAD HEART			

_____
(month)
KDRAMA MONTHLY LIST

Currently Watching

Top Three Favorite Kdramas
- ♥
- ♥
- ♥

K-dramas To Watch
- ♥
- ♥
- ♥
- ♥
- ♥
- ♥
- ♥
- ♥
- ♥

Favorite Oppa (Male Hero)

_____

(K-drama Title)

Date Started   Date Completed   Rating
⬜   ⬜   ★★★★★

Male Lead (Character Name/Actor Name)

Male Lead (Character Traits)
- ❤
- ❤
- ❤

Female Lead (Character Name/Actress Name)

Female Lead (Character Traits)
- ❤
- ❤
- ❤

Tropes

- ☐ gender switch
- ☐ reverse harem
- ☐ soul switching
- ☐ time travel
- ☐ memory loss
- ☐ opposite attract
- ☐ student/teacher
- ☐ secret baby
- ☐ May/December
- ☐ accidental pregnancy
- ☐ rich man (chaebol)
- ☐ actor/actress
- ☐ ghosts
- ☐ aliens
- ☐ murder case
- ☐ one night stand
- ☐ thriller
- ☐ Candy/Alpha
- ☐ historical
- ☐ brother's best friend
- ☐ fake relationship
- ☐ bromance
- ☐ childhood friends
- ☐ vampires
- ☐ fantasy
- ☐ workplace

_____

(K-drama Title)

Date Started

Date Completed

Rating
★★★★★

Male Lead (Character Name/Actor Name)

Male Lead (Character Traits)
- ♥
- ♥
- ♥

Female Lead (Character Name/Actress Name)

Female Lead (Character Traits)
- ♥
- ♥
- ♥

Tropes

- [ ] gender switch
- [ ] reverse harem
- [ ] soul switching
- [ ] time travel
- [ ] memory loss
- [ ] opposite attract
- [ ] student/teacher
- [ ] secret baby
- [ ] May/December
- [ ] accidental pregnancy
- [ ] rich man (chaebol)
- [ ] actor/actress
- [ ] ghosts
- [ ] aliens
- [ ] murder case
- [ ] one night stand
- [ ] thriller
- [ ] Candy/Alpha
- [ ] historical
- [ ] brother's best friend
- [ ] fake relationship
- [ ] bromance
- [ ] childhood friends
- [ ] vampires
- [ ] fantasy
- [ ] workplace

(K-drama Title)

Date Started

Date Completed

Rating
★★★★★

Male Lead (Character Name/Actor Name)

Male Lead (Character Traits)
- ♥
- ♥
- ♥

Female Lead (Character Name/Actress Name)

Female Lead (Character Traits)
- ♥
- ♥
- ♥

Tropes

- [ ] gender switch
- [ ] reverse harem
- [ ] soul switching
- [ ] time travel
- [ ] memory loss
- [ ] opposite attract
- [ ] student/teacher
- [ ] secret baby
- [ ] May/December
- [ ] accidental pregnancy
- [ ] rich man (chaebol)
- [ ] actor/actress
- [ ] ghosts
- [ ] aliens
- [ ] murder case
- [ ] one night stand
- [ ] thriller
- [ ] Candy/Alpha
- [ ] historical
- [ ] brother's best friend
- [ ] fake relationship
- [ ] bromance
- [ ] childhood friends
- [ ] vampires
- [ ] fantasy
- [ ] workplace
- [ ]
- [ ]
- [ ]
- [ ]

(K-drama Title)

Date Started

Date Completed

Rating
★★★★★

Male Lead (Character Name/Actor Name)

Male Lead (Character Traits)
- ♥
- ♥
- ♥

Female Lead (Character Name/Actress Name)

Female Lead (Character Traits)
- ♥
- ♥
- ♥

Tropes

- [ ] gender switch
- [ ] reverse harem
- [ ] soul switching
- [ ] time travel
- [ ] memory loss
- [ ] opposite attract
- [ ] student/teacher
- [ ] secret baby
- [ ] May/December
- [ ] accidental pregnancy
- [ ] rich man (chaebol)
- [ ] actor/actress
- [ ] ghosts
- [ ] aliens
- [ ] murder case
- [ ] one night stand
- [ ] thriller
- [ ] Candy/Alpha
- [ ] historical
- [ ] brother's best friend
- [ ] fake relationship
- [ ] bromance
- [ ] childhood friends
- [ ] vampires
- [ ] fantasy
- [ ] workplace

(K-drama Title)

Date Started **Date Completed** **Rating** ★★★★★

Male Lead (Character Name/Actor Name)

Male Lead (Character Traits)
- ♥
- ♥
- ♥

Female Lead (Character Name/Actress Name)

Female Lead (Character Traits)
- ♥
- ♥
- ♥

Tropes

- [ ] gender switch
- [ ] reverse harem
- [ ] soul switching
- [ ] time travel
- [ ] memory loss
- [ ] opposite attract
- [ ] student/teacher
- [ ] secret baby
- [ ] May/December
- [ ] accidental pregnancy
- [ ] rich man (chaebol)
- [ ] actor/actress
- [ ] ghosts
- [ ] aliens
- [ ] murder case
- [ ] one night stand
- [ ] thriller
- [ ] Candy/Alpha
- [ ] historical
- [ ] brother's best friend
- [ ] fake relationship
- [ ] bromance
- [ ] childhood friends
- [ ] vampires
- [ ] fantasy
- [ ] workplace
- [ ]
- [ ]
- [ ]
- [ ]

_____

(K-drama Title)

Date Started   Date Completed   Rating
★★★★★

Male Lead (Character Name/Actor Name)

Male Lead (Character Traits)
- ♥
- ♥
- ♥

Female Lead (Character Name/Actress Name)

Female Lead (Character Traits)
- ♥
- ♥
- ♥

Tropes

- [ ] gender switch
- [ ] reverse harem
- [ ] soul switching
- [ ] time travel
- [ ] memory loss
- [ ] opposite attract
- [ ] student/teacher
- [ ] secret baby
- [ ] May/December
- [ ] accidental pregnancy
- [ ] rich man (chaebol)
- [ ] actor/actress
- [ ] ghosts
- [ ] aliens
- [ ] murder case
- [ ] one night stand
- [ ] thriller
- [ ] Candy/Alpha
- [ ] historical
- [ ] brother's best friend
- [ ] fake relationship
- [ ] bromance
- [ ] childhood friends
- [ ] vampires
- [ ] fantasy
- [ ] workplace
- [ ]
- [ ]
- [ ]
- [ ]

K-DRAMA THIS OR THAT
AGE GAP

- [ ] HOTEL DEL LUNA
- [ ] SEARCH: WWW

- - - - - - - - - -

- [ ] YOU WHO CAME FROM THE STARS
- [ ] HOLD ME TIGHT

- - - - - - - - - -

- [ ] DOCTOR JOHN
- [ ] FIND ME IN YOUR MEMORY

- - - - - - - - - -

- [ ] HYENA
- [ ] WOMAN OF DIGNITY

- - - - - - - - - -

- [ ] MAMA
- [ ] MARRIAGE CONTRACT

(month)
KDRAMA MONTHLY LIST

Currently Watching

Top Three Favorite Kdramas
- ♥
- ♥
- ♥

K-dramas To Watch
- ♥
- ♥
- ♥
- ♥
- ♥
- ♥
- ♥
- ♥
- ♥

Favorite Oppa (Male Hero)

(K-drama Title)

Date Started **Date Completed** **Rating**
★★★★★

Male Lead (Character Name/Actor Name)

Male Lead (Character Traits)
- ♥
- ♥
- ♥

Female Lead (Character Name/Actress Name)

Female Lead (Character Traits)
- ♥
- ♥
- ♥

Tropes

- [ ] gender switch
- [ ] reverse harem
- [ ] soul switching
- [ ] time travel
- [ ] memory loss
- [ ] opposite attract
- [ ] student/teacher
- [ ] secret baby
- [ ] May/December
- [ ] accidental pregnancy
- [ ] rich man (chaebol)
- [ ] actor/actress
- [ ] ghosts
- [ ] aliens
- [ ] murder case
- [ ] one night stand
- [ ] thriller
- [ ] Candy/Alpha
- [ ] historical
- [ ] brother's best friend
- [ ] fake relationship
- [ ] bromance
- [ ] childhood friends
- [ ] vampires
- [ ] fantasy
- [ ] workplace
- [ ]
- [ ]
- [ ]
- [ ]

(K-drama Title)

Date Started

Date Completed

Rating
★★★★★

Male Lead (Character Name/Actor Name)

Male Lead (Character Traits)
- ♥
- ♥
- ♥

Female Lead (Character Name/Actress Name)

Female Lead (Character Traits)
- ♥
- ♥
- ♥

Tropes

- [ ] gender switch
- [ ] reverse harem
- [ ] soul switching
- [ ] time travel
- [ ] memory loss
- [ ] opposite attract
- [ ] student/teacher
- [ ] secret baby
- [ ] May/December
- [ ] accidental pregnancy
- [ ] rich man (chaebol)
- [ ] actor/actress
- [ ] ghosts
- [ ] aliens
- [ ] murder case
- [ ] one night stand
- [ ] thriller
- [ ] Candy/Alpha
- [ ] historical
- [ ] brother's best friend
- [ ] fake relationship
- [ ] bromance
- [ ] childhood friends
- [ ] vampires
- [ ] fantasy
- [ ] workplace
- [ ]
- [ ]
- [ ]
- [ ]

(K-drama Title)

Date Started

Date Completed

Rating
★★★★★

Male Lead (Character Name/Actor Name)

Male Lead (Character Traits)
- ♥
- ♥
- ♥

Female Lead (Character Name/Actress Name)

Female Lead (Character Traits)
- ♥
- ♥
- ♥

Tropes

- [ ] gender switch
- [ ] reverse harem
- [ ] soul switching
- [ ] time travel
- [ ] memory loss
- [ ] opposite attract
- [ ] student/teacher
- [ ] secret baby
- [ ] May/December
- [ ] accidental pregnancy
- [ ] rich man (chaebol)
- [ ] actor/actress
- [ ] ghosts
- [ ] aliens
- [ ] murder case
- [ ] one night stand
- [ ] thriller
- [ ] Candy/Alpha
- [ ] historical
- [ ] brother's best friend
- [ ] fake relationship
- [ ] bromance
- [ ] childhood friends
- [ ] vampires
- [ ] fantasy
- [ ] workplace
- [ ]
- [ ]
- [ ]
- [ ]

(K-drama Title)

Date Started

Date Completed

Rating
★★★★★

Male Lead (Character Name/Actor Name)

Male Lead (Character Traits)
- ♥
- ♥
- ♥

Female Lead (Character Name/Actress Name)

Female Lead (Character Traits)
- ♥
- ♥
- ♥

Tropes

- [ ] gender switch
- [ ] reverse harem
- [ ] soul switching
- [ ] time travel
- [ ] memory loss
- [ ] opposite attract
- [ ] student/teacher
- [ ] secret baby
- [ ] May/December
- [ ] accidental pregnancy
- [ ] rich man (chaebol)
- [ ] actor/actress
- [ ] ghosts
- [ ] aliens
- [ ] murder case
- [ ] one night stand
- [ ] thriller
- [ ] Candy/Alpha
- [ ] historical
- [ ] brother's best friend
- [ ] fake relationship
- [ ] bromance
- [ ] childhood friends
- [ ] vampires
- [ ] fantasy
- [ ] workplace

(K-drama Title)

Date Started   **Date Completed**   **Rating**
★★★★★

Male Lead (Character Name/Actor Name)

Male Lead (Character Traits)

- ♥
- ♥
- ♥

Female Lead (Character Name/Actress Name)

Female Lead (Character Traits)

- ♥
- ♥
- ♥

Tropes

- [ ] gender switch
- [ ] reverse harem
- [ ] soul switching
- [ ] time travel
- [ ] memory loss
- [ ] opposite attract
- [ ] student/teacher
- [ ] secret baby
- [ ] May/December
- [ ] accidental pregnancy
- [ ] rich man (chaebol)
- [ ] actor/actress
- [ ] ghosts
- [ ] aliens
- [ ] murder case
- [ ] one night stand
- [ ] thriller
- [ ] Candy/Alpha
- [ ] historical
- [ ] brother's best friend
- [ ] fake relationship
- [ ] bromance
- [ ] childhood friends
- [ ] vampires
- [ ] fantasy
- [ ] workplace
- [ ]
- [ ]
- [ ]
- [ ]

_____

(K-drama Title)

Date Started

Date Completed

Rating
★★★★★

Male Lead (Character Name/Actor Name)

Male Lead (Character Traits)

- ♥
- ♥
- ♥

Female Lead (Character Name/Actress Name)

Female Lead (Character Traits)

- ♥
- ♥
- ♥

Tropes

- ☐ gender switch
- ☐ reverse harem
- ☐ soul switching
- ☐ time travel
- ☐ memory loss
- ☐ opposite attract
- ☐ student/teacher
- ☐ secret baby
- ☐ May/December
- ☐ accidental pregnancy
- ☐ rich man (chaebol)
- ☐ actor/actress
- ☐ ghosts
- ☐ aliens
- ☐ murder case
- ☐ one night stand
- ☐ thriller
- ☐ Candy/Alpha
- ☐ historical
- ☐ brother's best friend
- ☐ fake relationship
- ☐ bromance
- ☐ childhood friends
- ☐ vampires
- ☐ fantasy
- ☐ workplace
- ☐
- ☐
- ☐
- ☐

MARRIAGE OF CONVENIENCE KDRAMA MASTER LIST

- ♥ FULL HOUSE
- ♥ I LOVE YOU
- ♥ HATEFUL BUT ONCE AGAIN
- ♥ JA MYUNG GO
- ♥ DANDELION FAMILY
- ♥ HAEUNDAE LOVERS
- ♥ QUEEN OF AMBITION
- ♥ FATED TO LOVE YOU
- ♥ MASK
- ♥ MARRIAGE CONTRACT
- ♥ TOMORROW WITH YOU
- ♥ BECAUSE THIS IS MY FIRST LIFE
- ♥ MONEY FLOWER
- ♥ HAPPY SISTERS
- ♥ 100 DAYS MY PRINCE
- ♥ GANGNAM SCANDAL
- ♥ BEAUTIFUL LOVE, WONDERFUL LIFE
- ♥ TOWER OF BABEL
- ♥ SEARCH: WWW

_____
(month)
KDRAMA MONTHLY LIST

Currently Watching

Top Three Favorite Kdramas
- ♥
- ♥
- ♥

K-dramas To Watch
- ♥
- ♥
- ♥
- ♥
- ♥
- ♥
- ♥
- ♥
- ♥

Favorite Oppa (Male Hero)

(K-drama Title)

Date Started

Date Completed

Rating
★★★★★

Male Lead (Character Name/Actor Name)

Male Lead (Character Traits)
- ❤
- ❤
- ❤

Female Lead (Character Name/Actress Name)

Female Lead (Character Traits)
- ❤
- ❤
- ❤

Tropes

- [ ] gender switch
- [ ] reverse harem
- [ ] soul switching
- [ ] time travel
- [ ] memory loss
- [ ] opposite attract
- [ ] student/teacher
- [ ] secret baby
- [ ] May/December
- [ ] accidental pregnancy
- [ ] rich man (chaebol)
- [ ] actor/actress
- [ ] ghosts
- [ ] aliens
- [ ] murder case
- [ ] one night stand
- [ ] thriller
- [ ] Candy/Alpha
- [ ] historical
- [ ] brother's best friend
- [ ] fake relationship
- [ ] bromance
- [ ] childhood friends
- [ ] vampires
- [ ] fantasy
- [ ] workplace

_____

(K-drama Title)

Date Started   Date Completed   Rating
★★★★★

Male Lead (Character Name/Actor Name)

Male Lead (Character Traits)
- ♥
- ♥
- ♥

Female Lead (Character Name/Actress Name)

Female Lead (Character Traits)
- ♥
- ♥
- ♥

Tropes

- [ ] gender switch
- [ ] reverse harem
- [ ] soul switching
- [ ] time travel
- [ ] memory loss
- [ ] opposite attract
- [ ] student/teacher
- [ ] secret baby
- [ ] May/December
- [ ] accidental pregnancy
- [ ] rich man (chaebol)
- [ ] actor/actress
- [ ] ghosts
- [ ] aliens
- [ ] murder case
- [ ] one night stand
- [ ] thriller
- [ ] Candy/Alpha
- [ ] historical
- [ ] brother's best friend
- [ ] fake relationship
- [ ] bromance
- [ ] childhood friends
- [ ] vampires
- [ ] fantasy
- [ ] workplace

_____

(K-drama Title)

Date Started

Date Completed

Rating
★★★★★

Male Lead (Character Name/Actor Name)

Male Lead (Character Traits)
- ♥
- ♥
- ♥

Female Lead (Character Name/Actress Name)

Female Lead (Character Traits)
- ♥
- ♥
- ♥

Tropes

- ☐ gender switch
- ☐ reverse harem
- ☐ soul switching
- ☐ time travel
- ☐ memory loss
- ☐ opposite attract
- ☐ student/teacher
- ☐ secret baby
- ☐ May/December
- ☐ accidental pregnancy
- ☐ rich man (chaebol)
- ☐ actor/actress
- ☐ ghosts
- ☐ aliens
- ☐ murder case
- ☐ one night stand
- ☐ thriller
- ☐ Candy/Alpha
- ☐ historical
- ☐ brother's best friend
- ☐ fake relationship
- ☐ bromance
- ☐ childhood friends
- ☐ vampires
- ☐ fantasy
- ☐ workplace
- ☐
- ☐
- ☐
- ☐

(K-drama Title)

Date Started **Date Completed** **Rating**
★★★★★

Male Lead (Character Name/Actor Name)

Male Lead (Character Traits)

- ♥
- ♥
- ♥

Female Lead (Character Name/Actress Name)

Female Lead (Character Traits)

- ♥
- ♥
- ♥

Tropes

- [ ] gender switch
- [ ] reverse harem
- [ ] soul switching
- [ ] time travel
- [ ] memory loss
- [ ] opposite attract
- [ ] student/teacher
- [ ] secret baby
- [ ] May/December
- [ ] accidental pregnancy
- [ ] rich man (chaebol)
- [ ] actor/actress
- [ ] ghosts
- [ ] aliens
- [ ] murder case
- [ ] one night stand
- [ ] thriller
- [ ] Candy/Alpha
- [ ] historical
- [ ] brother's best friend
- [ ] fake relationship
- [ ] bromance
- [ ] childhood friends
- [ ] vampires
- [ ] fantasy
- [ ] workplace
- [ ]
- [ ]
- [ ]
- [ ]

(K-drama Title)

Date Started

Date Completed

Rating
★★★★★

Male Lead (Character Name/Actor Name)

Male Lead (Character Traits)
- ♥
- ♥
- ♥

Female Lead (Character Name/Actress Name)

Female Lead (Character Traits)
- ♥
- ♥
- ♥

Tropes

☐ gender switch	☐ rich man (chaebol)	☐ fake relationship
☐ reverse harem	☐ actor/actress	☐ bromance
☐ soul switching	☐ ghosts	☐ childhood friends
☐ time travel	☐ aliens	☐ vampires
☐ memory loss	☐ murder case	☐ fantasy
☐ opposite attract	☐ one night stand	☐ workplace
☐ student/teacher	☐ thriller	☐
☐ secret baby	☐ Candy/Alpha	☐
☐ May/December	☐ historical	☐
☐ accidental pregnancy	☐ brother's best friend	☐

_____

(K-drama Title)

Date Started   Date Completed   Rating
⭐⭐⭐⭐⭐

Male Lead (Character Name/Actor Name)

Male Lead (Character Traits)

- ♥
- ♥
- ♥

Female Lead (Character Name/Actress Name)

Female Lead (Character Traits)

- ♥
- ♥
- ♥

Tropes

- ☐ gender switch
- ☐ reverse harem
- ☐ soul switching
- ☐ time travel
- ☐ memory loss
- ☐ opposite attract
- ☐ student/teacher
- ☐ secret baby
- ☐ May/December
- ☐ accidental pregnancy

- ☐ rich man (chaebol)
- ☐ actor/actress
- ☐ ghosts
- ☐ aliens
- ☐ murder case
- ☐ one night stand
- ☐ thriller
- ☐ Candy/Alpha
- ☐ historical
- ☐ brother's best friend

- ☐ fake relationship
- ☐ bromance
- ☐ childhood friends
- ☐ vampires
- ☐ fantasy
- ☐ workplace
- ☐
- ☐
- ☐
- ☐

K-DRAMA THIS OR THAT

TROPES

- [ ] CHAEBOL (rich dude)
- POLICE OFFICER [ ]

• • • • • • • • • •

- [ ] SECRET BABY
- SINGLE PARENT [ ]

• • • • • • • • • •

- [ ] VAMPIRES
- ALIENS [ ]

• • • • • • • • • •

- [ ] SOUL SWITCHING
- CONTRACT MARRIAGE [ ]

• • • • • • • • • •

- [ ] HIGH SCHOOL/TEEN
- WORKPLACE [ ]

(month)
KDRAMA MONTHLY LIST

Currently Watching

Top Three Favorite Kdramas
- ♥
- ♥
- ♥

K-dramas To Watch
- ♥
- ♥
- ♥
- ♥
- ♥
- ♥
- ♥
- ♥
- ♥

Favorite Oppa (Male Hero)

_____

(K-drama Title)

Date Started   Date Completed   Rating
☆☆☆☆☆

Male Lead (Character Name/Actor Name)

Male Lead (Character Traits)
- ♥
- ♥
- ♥

Female Lead (Character Name/Actress Name)

Female Lead (Character Traits)
- ♥
- ♥
- ♥

Tropes

- ☐ gender switch
- ☐ reverse harem
- ☐ soul switching
- ☐ time travel
- ☐ memory loss
- ☐ opposite attract
- ☐ student/teacher
- ☐ secret baby
- ☐ May/December
- ☐ accidental pregnancy
- ☐ rich man (chaebol)
- ☐ actor/actress
- ☐ ghosts
- ☐ aliens
- ☐ murder case
- ☐ one night stand
- ☐ thriller
- ☐ Candy/Alpha
- ☐ historical
- ☐ brother's best friend
- ☐ fake relationship
- ☐ bromance
- ☐ childhood friends
- ☐ vampires
- ☐ fantasy
- ☐ workplace
- ☐
- ☐
- ☐
- ☐

_____

(K-drama Title)

Date Started   Date Completed   Rating
☆☆☆☆☆

Male Lead (Character Name/Actor Name)

Male Lead (Character Traits)
- ♥
- ♥
- ♥

Female Lead (Character Name/Actress Name)

Female Lead (Character Traits)
- ♥
- ♥
- ♥

Tropes

- [ ] gender switch
- [ ] reverse harem
- [ ] soul switching
- [ ] time travel
- [ ] memory loss
- [ ] opposite attract
- [ ] student/teacher
- [ ] secret baby
- [ ] May/December
- [ ] accidental pregnancy
- [ ] rich man (chaebol)
- [ ] actor/actress
- [ ] ghosts
- [ ] aliens
- [ ] murder case
- [ ] one night stand
- [ ] thriller
- [ ] Candy/Alpha
- [ ] historical
- [ ] brother's best friend
- [ ] fake relationship
- [ ] bromance
- [ ] childhood friends
- [ ] vampires
- [ ] fantasy
- [ ] workplace
- [ ]
- [ ]
- [ ]
- [ ]

_____
(K-drama Title)

Date Started   Date Completed   Rating
★★★★★

Male Lead (Character Name/Actor Name)

Male Lead (Character Traits)
- ♥
- ♥
- ♥

Female Lead (Character Name/Actress Name)

Female Lead (Character Traits)
- ♥
- ♥
- ♥

Tropes

- [ ] gender switch
- [ ] reverse harem
- [ ] soul switching
- [ ] time travel
- [ ] memory loss
- [ ] opposite attract
- [ ] student/teacher
- [ ] secret baby
- [ ] May/December
- [ ] accidental pregnancy
- [ ] rich man (chaebol)
- [ ] actor/actress
- [ ] ghosts
- [ ] aliens
- [ ] murder case
- [ ] one night stand
- [ ] thriller
- [ ] Candy/Alpha
- [ ] historical
- [ ] brother's best friend
- [ ] fake relationship
- [ ] bromance
- [ ] childhood friends
- [ ] vampires
- [ ] fantasy
- [ ] workplace

_____

(K-drama Title)

Date Started   Date Completed   Rating
★★★★★

Male Lead (Character Name/Actor Name)

Male Lead (Character Traits)

- ♥
- ♥
- ♥

Female Lead (Character Name/Actress Name)

Female Lead (Character Traits)

- ♥
- ♥
- ♥

Tropes

- [ ] gender switch
- [ ] reverse harem
- [ ] soul switching
- [ ] time travel
- [ ] memory loss
- [ ] opposite attract
- [ ] student/teacher
- [ ] secret baby
- [ ] May/December
- [ ] accidental pregnancy
- [ ] rich man (chaebol)
- [ ] actor/actress
- [ ] ghosts
- [ ] aliens
- [ ] murder case
- [ ] one night stand
- [ ] thriller
- [ ] Candy/Alpha
- [ ] historical
- [ ] brother's best friend
- [ ] fake relationship
- [ ] bromance
- [ ] childhood friends
- [ ] vampires
- [ ] fantasy
- [ ] workplace
- [ ]
- [ ]
- [ ]
- [ ]

(K-drama Title)

Date Started | Date Completed | Rating
★★★★★

Male Lead (Character Name/Actor Name)

Male Lead (Character Traits)
- ♥
- ♥
- ♥

Female Lead (Character Name/Actress Name)

Female Lead (Character Traits)
- ♥
- ♥
- ♥

Tropes

- [ ] gender switch
- [ ] reverse harem
- [ ] soul switching
- [ ] time travel
- [ ] memory loss
- [ ] opposite attract
- [ ] student/teacher
- [ ] secret baby
- [ ] May/December
- [ ] accidental pregnancy
- [ ] rich man (chaebol)
- [ ] actor/actress
- [ ] ghosts
- [ ] aliens
- [ ] murder case
- [ ] one night stand
- [ ] thriller
- [ ] Candy/Alpha
- [ ] historical
- [ ] brother's best friend
- [ ] fake relationship
- [ ] bromance
- [ ] childhood friends
- [ ] vampires
- [ ] fantasy
- [ ] workplace

(K-drama Title)

Date Started

Date Completed

Rating ★★★★★

Male Lead (Character Name/Actor Name)

Male Lead (Character Traits)

- ♥
- ♥
- ♥

Female Lead (Character Name/Actress Name)

Female Lead (Character Traits)

- ♥
- ♥
- ♥

Tropes

- [ ] gender switch
- [ ] reverse harem
- [ ] soul switching
- [ ] time travel
- [ ] memory loss
- [ ] opposite attract
- [ ] student/teacher
- [ ] secret baby
- [ ] May/December
- [ ] accidental pregnancy
- [ ] rich man (chaebol)
- [ ] actor/actress
- [ ] ghosts
- [ ] aliens
- [ ] murder case
- [ ] one night stand
- [ ] thriller
- [ ] Candy/Alpha
- [ ] historical
- [ ] brother's best friend
- [ ] fake relationship
- [ ] bromance
- [ ] childhood friends
- [ ] vampires
- [ ] fantasy
- [ ] workplace
- [ ]
- [ ]
- [ ]
- [ ]

AMNESIA KDRAMA MASTER LIST

- ♥ THE LOVER
- ♥ FALLING FOR INNOCENCE
- ♥ LETS EAT 2
- ♥ WHO ARE YOU: SCHOOL 2015
- ♥ MY BEAUTIFUL BRIDE
- ♥ ALL ABOUT MY MOM
- ♥ D-DAY
- ♥ SIX FLYING DRAGONS
- ♥ SASSY GO GO
- ♥ REPLY 1988
- ♥ REMEMBER: WAR OF THE SON
- ♥ ONE MORE HAPPY ENDING
- ♥ FIVE ENOUGH
- ♥ PLEASE COME BACK, MISTER
- ♥ ABYSS
- ♥ MEMORY
- ♥ ANOTHER MISS OH
- ♥ A BEAUTIFUL MIND
- ♥ GO HO'S STARRY NIGHT
- ♥ W
- ♥ AGE OF YOUTH
- ♥ SHOPPING KING LOUIE
- ♥ THE K2

(month)

KDRAMA MONTHLY LIST

Currently Watching

Top Three Favorite Kdramas
- ♥
- ♥
- ♥

K-dramas To Watch
- ♥
- ♥
- ♥
- ♥
- ♥
- ♥
- ♥
- ♥
- ♥

Favorite Oppa (Male Hero)

_____

(K-drama Title)

Date Started　　Date Completed　　Rating
　　　　　　　　　　　　　　　　　　　★★★★★

Male Lead (Character Name/Actor Name)

Male Lead (Character Traits)
- ♥
- ♥
- ♥

Female Lead (Character Name/Actress Name)

Female Lead (Character Traits)
- ♥
- ♥
- ♥

Tropes

- [ ] gender switch
- [ ] reverse harem
- [ ] soul switching
- [ ] time travel
- [ ] memory loss
- [ ] opposite attract
- [ ] student/teacher
- [ ] secret baby
- [ ] May/December
- [ ] accidental pregnancy
- [ ] rich man (chaebol)
- [ ] actor/actress
- [ ] ghosts
- [ ] aliens
- [ ] murder case
- [ ] one night stand
- [ ] thriller
- [ ] Candy/Alpha
- [ ] historical
- [ ] brother's best friend
- [ ] fake relationship
- [ ] bromance
- [ ] childhood friends
- [ ] vampires
- [ ] fantasy
- [ ] workplace
- [ ]
- [ ]
- [ ]
- [ ]

(K-drama Title)

Date Started

Date Completed

Rating
★★★★★

Male Lead (Character Name/Actor Name)

Male Lead (Character Traits)

- ♥
- ♥
- ♥

Female Lead (Character Name/Actress Name)

Female Lead (Character Traits)

- ♥
- ♥
- ♥

Tropes

- [ ] gender switch
- [ ] reverse harem
- [ ] soul switching
- [ ] time travel
- [ ] memory loss
- [ ] opposite attract
- [ ] student/teacher
- [ ] secret baby
- [ ] May/December
- [ ] accidental pregnancy
- [ ] rich man (chaebol)
- [ ] actor/actress
- [ ] ghosts
- [ ] aliens
- [ ] murder case
- [ ] one night stand
- [ ] thriller
- [ ] Candy/Alpha
- [ ] historical
- [ ] brother's best friend
- [ ] fake relationship
- [ ] bromance
- [ ] childhood friends
- [ ] vampires
- [ ] fantasy
- [ ] workplace

_____

(K-drama Title)

Date Started   Date Completed   Rating
★★★★★

Male Lead (Character Name/Actor Name)

Male Lead (Character Traits)

- ♥
- ♥
- ♥

Female Lead (Character Name/Actress Name)

Female Lead (Character Traits)

- ♥
- ♥
- ♥

Tropes

- [ ] gender switch
- [ ] reverse harem
- [ ] soul switching
- [ ] time travel
- [ ] memory loss
- [ ] opposite attract
- [ ] student/teacher
- [ ] secret baby
- [ ] May/December
- [ ] accidental pregnancy
- [ ] rich man (chaebol)
- [ ] actor/actress
- [ ] ghosts
- [ ] aliens
- [ ] murder case
- [ ] one night stand
- [ ] thriller
- [ ] Candy/Alpha
- [ ] historical
- [ ] brother's best friend
- [ ] fake relationship
- [ ] bromance
- [ ] childhood friends
- [ ] vampires
- [ ] fantasy
- [ ] workplace

(K-drama Title)

Date Started   Date Completed   Rating
★★★★★

Male Lead (Character Name/Actor Name)

Male Lead (Character Traits)
- ♥
- ♥
- ♥

Female Lead (Character Name/Actress Name)

Female Lead (Character Traits)
- ♥
- ♥
- ♥

Tropes

- [ ] gender switch
- [ ] reverse harem
- [ ] soul switching
- [ ] time travel
- [ ] memory loss
- [ ] opposite attract
- [ ] student/teacher
- [ ] secret baby
- [ ] May/December
- [ ] accidental pregnancy
- [ ] rich man (chaebol)
- [ ] actor/actress
- [ ] ghosts
- [ ] aliens
- [ ] murder case
- [ ] one night stand
- [ ] thriller
- [ ] Candy/Alpha
- [ ] historical
- [ ] brother's best friend
- [ ] fake relationship
- [ ] bromance
- [ ] childhood friends
- [ ] vampires
- [ ] fantasy
- [ ] workplace

_____

(K-drama Title)

Date Started   Date Completed   Rating
★★★★★

Male Lead (Character Name/Actor Name)

Male Lead (Character Traits)

- ♥
- ♥
- ♥

Female Lead (Character Name/Actress Name)

Female Lead (Character Traits)

- ♥
- ♥
- ♥

Tropes

- ☐ gender switch
- ☐ reverse harem
- ☐ soul switching
- ☐ time travel
- ☐ memory loss
- ☐ opposite attract
- ☐ student/teacher
- ☐ secret baby
- ☐ May/December
- ☐ accidental pregnancy
- ☐ rich man (chaebol)
- ☐ actor/actress
- ☐ ghosts
- ☐ aliens
- ☐ murder case
- ☐ one night stand
- ☐ thriller
- ☐ Candy/Alpha
- ☐ historical
- ☐ brother's best friend
- ☐ fake relationship
- ☐ bromance
- ☐ childhood friends
- ☐ vampires
- ☐ fantasy
- ☐ workplace
- ☐
- ☐
- ☐
- ☐

_____

(K-drama Title)

Date Started   **Date Completed**   **Rating**
★★★★★

Male Lead (Character Name/Actor Name)

Male Lead (Character Traits)

- ♥
- ♥
- ♥

Female Lead (Character Name/Actress Name)

Female Lead (Character Traits)

- ♥
- ♥
- ♥

Tropes

- [ ] gender switch
- [ ] reverse harem
- [ ] soul switching
- [ ] time travel
- [ ] memory loss
- [ ] opposite attract
- [ ] student/teacher
- [ ] secret baby
- [ ] May/December
- [ ] accidental pregnancy
- [ ] rich man (chaebol)
- [ ] actor/actress
- [ ] ghosts
- [ ] aliens
- [ ] murder case
- [ ] one night stand
- [ ] thriller
- [ ] Candy/Alpha
- [ ] historical
- [ ] brother's best friend
- [ ] fake relationship
- [ ] bromance
- [ ] childhood friends
- [ ] vampires
- [ ] fantasy
- [ ] workplace
- [ ]
- [ ]
- [ ]
- [ ]

K-DRAMA THIS OR THAT

Oppa Edition

- [ ] LEE MIN HO / LEE JONG SUK [ ]
- [ ] JI CHANG WOOK / SONG JOONG KI [ ]
- [ ] KIM SOO HYUN / LEE JOON GI [ ]
- [ ] KIM WOO BIN / NAM JOO HYUK [ ]
- [ ] PARK SEO JOON / HYUN BIN [ ]
- [ ] SEO IN GUK / GONG YOO [ ]
- [ ] YOO SEUNG HO / PARK HYUNG SHIK [ ]

KDRAMA MONTHLY LIST
(month)

Currently Watching

Top Three Favorite Kdramas
- ♥
- ♥
- ♥

K-dramas To Watch
- ♥
- ♥
- ♥
- ♥
- ♥
- ♥
- ♥
- ♥
- ♥

Favorite Oppa (Male Hero)

_____

(K-drama Title)

Date Started   Date Completed   Rating
★★★★★

Male Lead (Character Name/Actor Name)

Male Lead (Character Traits)
- ♥
- ♥
- ♥

Female Lead (Character Name/Actress Name)

Female Lead (Character Traits)
- ♥
- ♥
- ♥

Tropes

- [ ] gender switch
- [ ] reverse harem
- [ ] soul switching
- [ ] time travel
- [ ] memory loss
- [ ] opposite attract
- [ ] student/teacher
- [ ] secret baby
- [ ] May/December
- [ ] accidental pregnancy
- [ ] rich man (chaebol)
- [ ] actor/actress
- [ ] ghosts
- [ ] aliens
- [ ] murder case
- [ ] one night stand
- [ ] thriller
- [ ] Candy/Alpha
- [ ] historical
- [ ] brother's best friend
- [ ] fake relationship
- [ ] bromance
- [ ] childhood friends
- [ ] vampires
- [ ] fantasy
- [ ] workplace
- [ ]
- [ ]
- [ ]
- [ ]

_____

(K-drama Title)

Date Started　　Date Completed　　Rating ★★★★★

Male Lead (Character Name/Actor Name)

Male Lead (Character Traits)

- ♥
- ♥
- ♥

Female Lead (Character Name/Actress Name)

Female Lead (Character Traits)

- ♥
- ♥
- ♥

Tropes

- [ ] gender switch
- [ ] reverse harem
- [ ] soul switching
- [ ] time travel
- [ ] memory loss
- [ ] opposite attract
- [ ] student/teacher
- [ ] secret baby
- [ ] May/December
- [ ] accidental pregnancy
- [ ] rich man (chaebol)
- [ ] actor/actress
- [ ] ghosts
- [ ] aliens
- [ ] murder case
- [ ] one night stand
- [ ] thriller
- [ ] Candy/Alpha
- [ ] historical
- [ ] brother's best friend
- [ ] fake relationship
- [ ] bromance
- [ ] childhood friends
- [ ] vampires
- [ ] fantasy
- [ ] workplace

_____

(K-drama Title)

Date Started　　Date Completed　　Rating
　　　　　　　　　　　　　　　　　　★★★★★

Male Lead (Character Name/Actor Name)

Male Lead (Character Traits)

- ♥
- ♥
- ♥

Female Lead (Character Name/Actress Name)

Female Lead (Character Traits)

- ♥
- ♥
- ♥

Tropes

- [ ] gender switch
- [ ] reverse harem
- [ ] soul switching
- [ ] time travel
- [ ] memory loss
- [ ] opposite attract
- [ ] student/teacher
- [ ] secret baby
- [ ] May/December
- [ ] accidental pregnancy
- [ ] rich man (chaebol)
- [ ] actor/actress
- [ ] ghosts
- [ ] aliens
- [ ] murder case
- [ ] one night stand
- [ ] thriller
- [ ] Candy/Alpha
- [ ] historical
- [ ] brother's best friend
- [ ] fake relationship
- [ ] bromance
- [ ] childhood friends
- [ ] vampires
- [ ] fantasy
- [ ] workplace
- [ ]
- [ ]
- [ ]
- [ ]

_____

(K-drama Title)

Date Started   Date Completed   Rating
⭐⭐⭐⭐⭐

Male Lead (Character Name/Actor Name)

Male Lead (Character Traits)
- ♥
- ♥
- ♥

Female Lead (Character Name/Actress Name)

Female Lead (Character Traits)
- ♥
- ♥
- ♥

Tropes

- [ ] gender switch
- [ ] reverse harem
- [ ] soul switching
- [ ] time travel
- [ ] memory loss
- [ ] opposite attract
- [ ] student/teacher
- [ ] secret baby
- [ ] May/December
- [ ] accidental pregnancy
- [ ] rich man (chaebol)
- [ ] actor/actress
- [ ] ghosts
- [ ] aliens
- [ ] murder case
- [ ] one night stand
- [ ] thriller
- [ ] Candy/Alpha
- [ ] historical
- [ ] brother's best friend
- [ ] fake relationship
- [ ] bromance
- [ ] childhood friends
- [ ] vampires
- [ ] fantasy
- [ ] workplace

(K-drama Title)

Date Started

Date Completed

Rating
★★★★★

Male Lead (Character Name/Actor Name)

Male Lead (Character Traits)
- ♥
- ♥
- ♥

Female Lead (Character Name/Actress Name)

Female Lead (Character Traits)
- ♥
- ♥
- ♥

Tropes

- [ ] gender switch
- [ ] reverse harem
- [ ] soul switching
- [ ] time travel
- [ ] memory loss
- [ ] opposite attract
- [ ] student/teacher
- [ ] secret baby
- [ ] May/December
- [ ] accidental pregnancy
- [ ] rich man (chaebol)
- [ ] actor/actress
- [ ] ghosts
- [ ] aliens
- [ ] murder case
- [ ] one night stand
- [ ] thriller
- [ ] Candy/Alpha
- [ ] historical
- [ ] brother's best friend
- [ ] fake relationship
- [ ] bromance
- [ ] childhood friends
- [ ] vampires
- [ ] fantasy
- [ ] workplace
- [ ]
- [ ]
- [ ]
- [ ]

_____

(K-drama Title)

Date Started   **Date Completed**   **Rating**
⭐⭐⭐⭐⭐

Male Lead (Character Name/Actor Name)

Male Lead (Character Traits)

- ♥
- ♥
- ♥

Female Lead (Character Name/Actress Name)

Female Lead (Character Traits)

- ♥
- ♥
- ♥

Tropes

- [ ] gender switch
- [ ] reverse harem
- [ ] soul switching
- [ ] time travel
- [ ] memory loss
- [ ] opposite attract
- [ ] student/teacher
- [ ] secret baby
- [ ] May/December
- [ ] accidental pregnancy
- [ ] rich man (chaebol)
- [ ] actor/actress
- [ ] ghosts
- [ ] aliens
- [ ] murder case
- [ ] one night stand
- [ ] thriller
- [ ] Candy/Alpha
- [ ] historical
- [ ] brother's best friend
- [ ] fake relationship
- [ ] bromance
- [ ] childhood friends
- [ ] vampires
- [ ] fantasy
- [ ] workplace
- [ ]
- [ ]
- [ ]
- [ ]

NETFLIX KDRAMA MASTER LIST

- ♥ MY ONLY LOVE SONG ★★★★★
- ♥ A KOREAN ODYSSEY ★★★★★
- ♥ LIVE ★★★★★
- ♥ SOMETHING IN THE RAIN ★★★★★
- ♥ MR. SUNSHINE ★★★★★
- ♥ THE HYMN OF DEATH ★★★★★
- ♥ MEMORIES OF ALHAMBRA ★★★★★
- ♥ ROMANCE IS A BONUS BOOK ★★★★★
- ♥ MY FIRST FIRST LOVE ★★★★★
- ♥ ONE SPRING NIGHT ★★★★★
- ♥ ARTHDAL CHRONICLES ★★★★★
- ♥ ROOKIE HISTORIAN GOO HAE RYUNG ★★★★★
- ♥ LOVE ALARM ★★★★★
- ♥ WHEN THE CAMELLIA BLOOMS ★★★★★
- ♥ MY COUNTRY: THE NEW AGE ★★★★★
- ♥ CHOCOLATE ★★★★★
- ♥ CRASH LANDING ON YOU ★★★★★
- ♥ ITAEWON CLASS ★★★★★
- ♥ MY HOLO LOVE ★★★★★
- ♥ HYENA ★★★★★
- ♥ HI BYE, MAMA! ★★★★★
- ♥ HOSPITAL PLAYLIST ★★★★★
- ♥ THE KING: ETERNAL MONARCH ★★★★★

_____
(month)
KDRAMA MONTHLY LIST

Currently Watching

Top Three Favorite Kdramas
- ♥
- ♥
- ♥

K-dramas To Watch
- ♥
- ♥
- ♥
- ♥
- ♥
- ♥
- ♥
- ♥
- ♥

Favorite Oppa (Male Hero)

_____

(K-drama Title)

Date Started

Date Completed

Rating
★★★★★

Male Lead (Character Name/Actor Name)

Male Lead (Character Traits)
- ♥
- ♥
- ♥

Female Lead (Character Name/Actress Name)

Female Lead (Character Traits)
- ♥
- ♥
- ♥

Tropes

- [ ] gender switch
- [ ] reverse harem
- [ ] soul switching
- [ ] time travel
- [ ] memory loss
- [ ] opposite attract
- [ ] student/teacher
- [ ] secret baby
- [ ] May/December
- [ ] accidental pregnancy
- [ ] rich man (chaebol)
- [ ] actor/actress
- [ ] ghosts
- [ ] aliens
- [ ] murder case
- [ ] one night stand
- [ ] thriller
- [ ] Candy/Alpha
- [ ] historical
- [ ] brother's best friend
- [ ] fake relationship
- [ ] bromance
- [ ] childhood friends
- [ ] vampires
- [ ] fantasy
- [ ] workplace
- [ ]
- [ ]
- [ ]
- [ ]

(K-drama Title)

Date Started   Date Completed   Rating
⭐⭐⭐⭐⭐

Male Lead (Character Name/Actor Name)

Male Lead (Character Traits)
- ♥
- ♥
- ♥

Female Lead (Character Name/Actress Name)

Female Lead (Character Traits)
- ♥
- ♥
- ♥

Tropes

- [ ] gender switch
- [ ] reverse harem
- [ ] soul switching
- [ ] time travel
- [ ] memory loss
- [ ] opposite attract
- [ ] student/teacher
- [ ] secret baby
- [ ] May/December
- [ ] accidental pregnancy
- [ ] rich man (chaebol)
- [ ] actor/actress
- [ ] ghosts
- [ ] aliens
- [ ] murder case
- [ ] one night stand
- [ ] thriller
- [ ] Candy/Alpha
- [ ] historical
- [ ] brother's best friend
- [ ] fake relationship
- [ ] bromance
- [ ] childhood friends
- [ ] vampires
- [ ] fantasy
- [ ] workplace
- [ ]
- [ ]
- [ ]
- [ ]

_____
(K-drama Title)

Date Started   Date Completed   Rating
⭐⭐⭐⭐⭐

Male Lead (Character Name/Actor Name)

Male Lead (Character Traits)
- ♥
- ♥
- ♥

Female Lead (Character Name/Actress Name)

Female Lead (Character Traits)
- ♥
- ♥
- ♥

Tropes

- [ ] gender switch
- [ ] reverse harem
- [ ] soul switching
- [ ] time travel
- [ ] memory loss
- [ ] opposite attract
- [ ] student/teacher
- [ ] secret baby
- [ ] May/December
- [ ] accidental pregnancy
- [ ] rich man (chaebol)
- [ ] actor/actress
- [ ] ghosts
- [ ] aliens
- [ ] murder case
- [ ] one night stand
- [ ] thriller
- [ ] Candy/Alpha
- [ ] historical
- [ ] brother's best friend
- [ ] fake relationship
- [ ] bromance
- [ ] childhood friends
- [ ] vampires
- [ ] fantasy
- [ ] workplace
- [ ]
- [ ]
- [ ]
- [ ]

(K-drama Title)

Date Started

Date Completed

Rating
★★★★★

Male Lead (Character Name/Actor Name)

Male Lead (Character Traits)
- ♥
- ♥
- ♥

Female Lead (Character Name/Actress Name)

Female Lead (Character Traits)
- ♥
- ♥
- ♥

Tropes

- [ ] gender switch
- [ ] reverse harem
- [ ] soul switching
- [ ] time travel
- [ ] memory loss
- [ ] opposite attract
- [ ] student/teacher
- [ ] secret baby
- [ ] May/December
- [ ] accidental pregnancy
- [ ] rich man (chaebol)
- [ ] actor/actress
- [ ] ghosts
- [ ] aliens
- [ ] murder case
- [ ] one night stand
- [ ] thriller
- [ ] Candy/Alpha
- [ ] historical
- [ ] brother's best friend
- [ ] fake relationship
- [ ] bromance
- [ ] childhood friends
- [ ] vampires
- [ ] fantasy
- [ ] workplace
- [ ]
- [ ]
- [ ]
- [ ]

(K-drama Title)

Date Started   Date Completed   Rating
★★★★★

Male Lead (Character Name/Actor Name)

Male Lead (Character Traits)
- ♥
- ♥
- ♥

Female Lead (Character Name/Actress Name)

Female Lead (Character Traits)
- ♥
- ♥
- ♥

Tropes

- [ ] gender switch
- [ ] reverse harem
- [ ] soul switching
- [ ] time travel
- [ ] memory loss
- [ ] opposite attract
- [ ] student/teacher
- [ ] secret baby
- [ ] May/December
- [ ] accidental pregnancy
- [ ] rich man (chaebol)
- [ ] actor/actress
- [ ] ghosts
- [ ] aliens
- [ ] murder case
- [ ] one night stand
- [ ] thriller
- [ ] Candy/Alpha
- [ ] historical
- [ ] brother's best friend
- [ ] fake relationship
- [ ] bromance
- [ ] childhood friends
- [ ] vampires
- [ ] fantasy
- [ ] workplace

(K-drama Title)

Date Started

Date Completed

Rating
★★★★★

Male Lead (Character Name/Actor Name)

Male Lead (Character Traits)
- ♥
- ♥
- ♥

Female Lead (Character Name/Actress Name)

Female Lead (Character Traits)
- ♥
- ♥
- ♥

Tropes

- [ ] gender switch
- [ ] reverse harem
- [ ] soul switching
- [ ] time travel
- [ ] memory loss
- [ ] opposite attract
- [ ] student/teacher
- [ ] secret baby
- [ ] May/December
- [ ] accidental pregnancy
- [ ] rich man (chaebol)
- [ ] actor/actress
- [ ] ghosts
- [ ] aliens
- [ ] murder case
- [ ] one night stand
- [ ] thriller
- [ ] Candy/Alpha
- [ ] historical
- [ ] brother's best friend
- [ ] fake relationship
- [ ] bromance
- [ ] childhood friends
- [ ] vampires
- [ ] fantasy
- [ ] workplace
- [ ]
- [ ]
- [ ]
- [ ]

K-DRAMA THIS OR THAT

Best Bromance

- [ ] GOBLIN
- [ ] CITY HUNTER

• • • • • • • • • •

- [ ] COFFEE PRINCE
- [ ] DESCENDANTS OF THE SUN

• • • • • • • • • •

- [ ] STRONG WOMAN DO BONG SOON
- [ ] KILL ME, HEAL ME

• • • • • • • • • •

- [ ] PINOCCHIO
- [ ] MOON LOVERS, SCARLET HEART RYEO

• • • • • • • • • •

- [ ] SECRET GARDEN
- [ ] WHILE YOU WERE SLEEPING

_____
(month)
KDRAMA MONTHLY LIST

Currently Watching

Top Three Favorite Kdramas
- ♥
- ♥
- ♥

K-dramas To Watch
- ♥
- ♥
- ♥
- ♥
- ♥
- ♥
- ♥
- ♥
- ♥

Favorite Oppa (Male Hero)

_____
(K-drama Title)

Date Started   Date Completed   Rating
★★★★★

Male Lead (Character Name/Actor Name)

Male Lead (Character Traits)
- ♥
- ♥
- ♥

Female Lead (Character Name/Actress Name)

Female Lead (Character Traits)
- ♥
- ♥
- ♥

Tropes

- [ ] gender switch
- [ ] reverse harem
- [ ] soul switching
- [ ] time travel
- [ ] memory loss
- [ ] opposite attract
- [ ] student/teacher
- [ ] secret baby
- [ ] May/December
- [ ] accidental pregnancy
- [ ] rich man (chaebol)
- [ ] actor/actress
- [ ] ghosts
- [ ] aliens
- [ ] murder case
- [ ] one night stand
- [ ] thriller
- [ ] Candy/Alpha
- [ ] historical
- [ ] brother's best friend
- [ ] fake relationship
- [ ] bromance
- [ ] childhood friends
- [ ] vampires
- [ ] fantasy
- [ ] workplace

(K-drama Title)

Date Started

Date Completed

Rating
★★★★★

Male Lead (Character Name/Actor Name)

Male Lead (Character Traits)
- ♥
- ♥
- ♥

Female Lead (Character Name/Actress Name)

Female Lead (Character Traits)
- ♥
- ♥
- ♥

Tropes

- [ ] gender switch
- [ ] reverse harem
- [ ] soul switching
- [ ] time travel
- [ ] memory loss
- [ ] opposite attract
- [ ] student/teacher
- [ ] secret baby
- [ ] May/December
- [ ] accidental pregnancy
- [ ] rich man (chaebol)
- [ ] actor/actress
- [ ] ghosts
- [ ] aliens
- [ ] murder case
- [ ] one night stand
- [ ] thriller
- [ ] Candy/Alpha
- [ ] historical
- [ ] brother's best friend
- [ ] fake relationship
- [ ] bromance
- [ ] childhood friends
- [ ] vampires
- [ ] fantasy
- [ ] workplace

(K-drama Title)

Date Started

Date Completed

Rating
★★★★★

Male Lead (Character Name/Actor Name)

Male Lead (Character Traits)
- ♥
- ♥
- ♥

Female Lead (Character Name/Actress Name)

Female Lead (Character Traits)
- ♥
- ♥
- ♥

Tropes

- [ ] gender switch
- [ ] reverse harem
- [ ] soul switching
- [ ] time travel
- [ ] memory loss
- [ ] opposite attract
- [ ] student/teacher
- [ ] secret baby
- [ ] May/December
- [ ] accidental pregnancy
- [ ] rich man (chaebol)
- [ ] actor/actress
- [ ] ghosts
- [ ] aliens
- [ ] murder case
- [ ] one night stand
- [ ] thriller
- [ ] Candy/Alpha
- [ ] historical
- [ ] brother's best friend
- [ ] fake relationship
- [ ] bromance
- [ ] childhood friends
- [ ] vampires
- [ ] fantasy
- [ ] workplace

_____

(K-drama Title)

Date Started   Date Completed   Rating
⭐⭐⭐⭐⭐

Male Lead (Character Name/Actor Name)

Male Lead (Character Traits)
- ♥
- ♥
- ♥

Female Lead (Character Name/Actress Name)

Female Lead (Character Traits)
- ♥
- ♥
- ♥

Tropes

- [ ] gender switch
- [ ] reverse harem
- [ ] soul switching
- [ ] time travel
- [ ] memory loss
- [ ] opposite attract
- [ ] student/teacher
- [ ] secret baby
- [ ] May/December
- [ ] accidental pregnancy
- [ ] rich man (chaebol)
- [ ] actor/actress
- [ ] ghosts
- [ ] aliens
- [ ] murder case
- [ ] one night stand
- [ ] thriller
- [ ] Candy/Alpha
- [ ] historical
- [ ] brother's best friend
- [ ] fake relationship
- [ ] bromance
- [ ] childhood friends
- [ ] vampires
- [ ] fantasy
- [ ] workplace
- [ ]
- [ ]
- [ ]
- [ ]

_____

(K-drama Title)

Date Started

Date Completed

Rating
★★★★★

Male Lead (Character Name/Actor Name)

Male Lead (Character Traits)
- ♥
- ♥
- ♥

Female Lead (Character Name/Actress Name)

Female Lead (Character Traits)
- ♥
- ♥
- ♥

Tropes

- [ ] gender switch
- [ ] reverse harem
- [ ] soul switching
- [ ] time travel
- [ ] memory loss
- [ ] opposite attract
- [ ] student/teacher
- [ ] secret baby
- [ ] May/December
- [ ] accidental pregnancy
- [ ] rich man (chaebol)
- [ ] actor/actress
- [ ] ghosts
- [ ] aliens
- [ ] murder case
- [ ] one night stand
- [ ] thriller
- [ ] Candy/Alpha
- [ ] historical
- [ ] brother's best friend
- [ ] fake relationship
- [ ] bromance
- [ ] childhood friends
- [ ] vampires
- [ ] fantasy
- [ ] workplace
- [ ]
- [ ]
- [ ]
- [ ]

(K-drama Title)

Date Started Date Completed Rating
★★★★★

Male Lead (Character Name/Actor Name)

Male Lead (Character Traits)
- ♥
- ♥
- ♥

Female Lead (Character Name/Actress Name)

Female Lead (Character Traits)
- ♥
- ♥
- ♥

Tropes

- [ ] gender switch
- [ ] reverse harem
- [ ] soul switching
- [ ] time travel
- [ ] memory loss
- [ ] opposite attract
- [ ] student/teacher
- [ ] secret baby
- [ ] May/December
- [ ] accidental pregnancy

- [ ] rich man (chaebol)
- [ ] actor/actress
- [ ] ghosts
- [ ] aliens
- [ ] murder case
- [ ] one night stand
- [ ] thriller
- [ ] Candy/Alpha
- [ ] historical
- [ ] brother's best friend

- [ ] fake relationship
- [ ] bromance
- [ ] childhood friends
- [ ] vampires
- [ ] fantasy
- [ ] workplace
- [ ]
- [ ]
- [ ]
- [ ]

VIKI KDRAMA MASTER LIST

- ♥ LOVE CELLS
- ♥ DRAMAWORLD
- ♥ THE KING IN LOVE
- ♥ MELOHOLIC
- ♥ SHORT
- ♥ GRAND PRINCE
- ♥ RICH MAN
- ♥ WITCH'S LOVE
- ♥ DEVILISH JOY
- ♥ WHERE STARS LAND
- ♥ TWELVE NIGHTS
- ♥ FLUTTERING WARNING
- ♥ I PICKED UP A STAR ON THE ROAD
- ♥ FATES & FURIES
- ♥ COFFEE, DO ME A FAVOR
- ♥ BEST CHICKEN
- ♥ WIND-BELL
- ♥ TOWER OF BABEL
- ♥ THE LIGHT IN YOUR EYES
- ♥ I HATE YOU JULIET
- ♥ MY ABSOLUTE BOYFRIEND
- ♥ LEVEL UP
- ♥ MOMENT AT EIGHTEEN
- ♥ BE MELODRAMATIC
- ♥ FLOWER CREW: JOSEON MARRIAGE AGENCY

_____
(month)
KDRAMA MONTHLY LIST

Currently Watching

Top Three Favorite Kdramas
- ♥
- ♥
- ♥

K-dramas To Watch
- ♥
- ♥
- ♥
- ♥
- ♥
- ♥
- ♥
- ♥
- ♥

Favorite Oppa (Male Hero)

_____

(K-drama Title)

Date Started   Date Completed   Rating
★★★★★

Male Lead (Character Name/Actor Name)

Male Lead (Character Traits)
- ♥
- ♥
- ♥

Female Lead (Character Name/Actress Name)

Female Lead (Character Traits)
- ♥
- ♥
- ♥

Tropes

- [ ] gender switch
- [ ] reverse harem
- [ ] soul switching
- [ ] time travel
- [ ] memory loss
- [ ] opposite attract
- [ ] student/teacher
- [ ] secret baby
- [ ] May/December
- [ ] accidental pregnancy
- [ ] rich man (chaebol)
- [ ] actor/actress
- [ ] ghosts
- [ ] aliens
- [ ] murder case
- [ ] one night stand
- [ ] thriller
- [ ] Candy/Alpha
- [ ] historical
- [ ] brother's best friend
- [ ] fake relationship
- [ ] bromance
- [ ] childhood friends
- [ ] vampires
- [ ] fantasy
- [ ] workplace

(K-drama Title)

Date Started **Date Completed** **Rating**
★★★★★

Male Lead (Character Name/Actor Name)

Male Lead (Character Traits)
- ♥
- ♥
- ♥

Female Lead (Character Name/Actress Name)

Female Lead (Character Traits)
- ♥
- ♥
- ♥

Tropes

- [ ] gender switch
- [ ] reverse harem
- [ ] soul switching
- [ ] time travel
- [ ] memory loss
- [ ] opposite attract
- [ ] student/teacher
- [ ] secret baby
- [ ] May/December
- [ ] accidental pregnancy
- [ ] rich man (chaebol)
- [ ] actor/actress
- [ ] ghosts
- [ ] aliens
- [ ] murder case
- [ ] one night stand
- [ ] thriller
- [ ] Candy/Alpha
- [ ] historical
- [ ] brother's best friend
- [ ] fake relationship
- [ ] bromance
- [ ] childhood friends
- [ ] vampires
- [ ] fantasy
- [ ] workplace
- [ ]
- [ ]
- [ ]
- [ ]

_____

(K-drama Title)

Date Started

Date Completed

Rating
★★★★★

Male Lead (Character Name/Actor Name)

Male Lead (Character Traits)
- ♥
- ♥
- ♥

Female Lead (Character Name/Actress Name)

Female Lead (Character Traits)
- ♥
- ♥
- ♥

Tropes

- [ ] gender switch
- [ ] reverse harem
- [ ] soul switching
- [ ] time travel
- [ ] memory loss
- [ ] opposite attract
- [ ] student/teacher
- [ ] secret baby
- [ ] May/December
- [ ] accidental pregnancy
- [ ] rich man (chaebol)
- [ ] actor/actress
- [ ] ghosts
- [ ] aliens
- [ ] murder case
- [ ] one night stand
- [ ] thriller
- [ ] Candy/Alpha
- [ ] historical
- [ ] brother's best friend
- [ ] fake relationship
- [ ] bromance
- [ ] childhood friends
- [ ] vampires
- [ ] fantasy
- [ ] workplace
- [ ]
- [ ]
- [ ]
- [ ]

_____

(K-drama Title)

Date Started   Date Completed   Rating
★★★★★

Male Lead (Character Name/Actor Name)

Male Lead (Character Traits)
- ♥
- ♥
- ♥

Female Lead (Character Name/Actress Name)

Female Lead (Character Traits)
- ♥
- ♥
- ♥

Tropes

- [ ] gender switch
- [ ] reverse harem
- [ ] soul switching
- [ ] time travel
- [ ] memory loss
- [ ] opposite attract
- [ ] student/teacher
- [ ] secret baby
- [ ] May/December
- [ ] accidental pregnancy
- [ ] rich man (chaebol)
- [ ] actor/actress
- [ ] ghosts
- [ ] aliens
- [ ] murder case
- [ ] one night stand
- [ ] thriller
- [ ] Candy/Alpha
- [ ] historical
- [ ] brother's best friend
- [ ] fake relationship
- [ ] bromance
- [ ] childhood friends
- [ ] vampires
- [ ] fantasy
- [ ] workplace

_____

(K-drama Title)

Date Started | Date Completed | Rating
⭐⭐⭐⭐⭐

Male Lead (Character Name/Actor Name)

Male Lead (Character Traits)

- ❤
- ❤
- ❤

Female Lead (Character Name/Actress Name)

Female Lead (Character Traits)

- ❤
- ❤
- ❤

Tropes

- [ ] gender switch
- [ ] reverse harem
- [ ] soul switching
- [ ] time travel
- [ ] memory loss
- [ ] opposite attract
- [ ] student/teacher
- [ ] secret baby
- [ ] May/December
- [ ] accidental pregnancy
- [ ] rich man (chaebol)
- [ ] actor/actress
- [ ] ghosts
- [ ] aliens
- [ ] murder case
- [ ] one night stand
- [ ] thriller
- [ ] Candy/Alpha
- [ ] historical
- [ ] brother's best friend
- [ ] fake relationship
- [ ] bromance
- [ ] childhood friends
- [ ] vampires
- [ ] fantasy
- [ ] workplace
- [ ]
- [ ]
- [ ]
- [ ]

_____

(K-drama Title)

Date Started Date Completed Rating
★★★★★

Male Lead (Character Name/Actor Name)

Male Lead (Character Traits)

- ♥
- ♥
- ♥

Female Lead (Character Name/Actress Name)

Female Lead (Character Traits)

- ♥
- ♥
- ♥

Tropes

- [ ] gender switch
- [ ] reverse harem
- [ ] soul switching
- [ ] time travel
- [ ] memory loss
- [ ] opposite attract
- [ ] student/teacher
- [ ] secret baby
- [ ] May/December
- [ ] accidental pregnancy
- [ ] rich man (chaebol)
- [ ] actor/actress
- [ ] ghosts
- [ ] aliens
- [ ] murder case
- [ ] one night stand
- [ ] thriller
- [ ] Candy/Alpha
- [ ] historical
- [ ] brother's best friend
- [ ] fake relationship
- [ ] bromance
- [ ] childhood friends
- [ ] vampires
- [ ] fantasy
- [ ] workplace

K-DRAMA THIS OR THAT

Best Friends to Lovers

- [ ] WEIGHTLIFTING FAIRY KIM BOK JOO
- ROMANCE IS A BONUS BOOK [ ]

- - - - - - - - - -

- [ ] EULACHACHA WAIKIKI
- REPLY 1997 [ ]

- - - - - - - - - -

- [ ] FIGHT FOR MY WAY
- ITAEWON CLASS [ ]

- - - - - - - - - -

- [ ] EXTRAORDINARY YOU
- MY ID IS GANGNAM BEAUTY [ ]

- - - - - - - - - -

- [ ] THE SMILE HAS LEFT YOUR EYES
- COME AND HUG ME [ ]

(month)

KDRAMA MONTHLY LIST

Currently Watching

Top Three Favorite Kdramas
- ♥
- ♥
- ♥

K-dramas To Watch
- ♥
- ♥
- ♥
- ♥
- ♥
- ♥
- ♥
- ♥
- ♥

Favorite Oppa (Male Hero)

(K-drama Title)

Date Started **Date Completed** **Rating** ★★★★★

Male Lead (Character Name/Actor Name)

Male Lead (Character Traits)
- ♥
- ♥
- ♥

Female Lead (Character Name/Actress Name)

Female Lead (Character Traits)
- ♥
- ♥
- ♥

Tropes

- [ ] gender switch
- [ ] reverse harem
- [ ] soul switching
- [ ] time travel
- [ ] memory loss
- [ ] opposite attract
- [ ] student/teacher
- [ ] secret baby
- [ ] May/December
- [ ] accidental pregnancy
- [ ] rich man (chaebol)
- [ ] actor/actress
- [ ] ghosts
- [ ] aliens
- [ ] murder case
- [ ] one night stand
- [ ] thriller
- [ ] Candy/Alpha
- [ ] historical
- [ ] brother's best friend
- [ ] fake relationship
- [ ] bromance
- [ ] childhood friends
- [ ] vampires
- [ ] fantasy
- [ ] workplace

_____

(K-drama Title)

Date Started   Date Completed   Rating

★★★★★

Male Lead (Character Name/Actor Name)

Male Lead (Character Traits)

- ♥
- ♥
- ♥

Female Lead (Character Name/Actress Name)

Female Lead (Character Traits)

- ♥
- ♥
- ♥

Tropes

- [ ] gender switch
- [ ] reverse harem
- [ ] soul switching
- [ ] time travel
- [ ] memory loss
- [ ] opposite attract
- [ ] student/teacher
- [ ] secret baby
- [ ] May/December
- [ ] accidental pregnancy
- [ ] rich man (chaebol)
- [ ] actor/actress
- [ ] ghosts
- [ ] aliens
- [ ] murder case
- [ ] one night stand
- [ ] thriller
- [ ] Candy/Alpha
- [ ] historical
- [ ] brother's best friend
- [ ] fake relationship
- [ ] bromance
- [ ] childhood friends
- [ ] vampires
- [ ] fantasy
- [ ] workplace

(K-drama Title)

Date Started

Date Completed

Rating
★★★★★

Male Lead (Character Name/Actor Name)

Male Lead (Character Traits)
- ♥
- ♥
- ♥

Female Lead (Character Name/Actress Name)

Female Lead (Character Traits)
- ♥
- ♥
- ♥

Tropes

- [ ] gender switch
- [ ] reverse harem
- [ ] soul switching
- [ ] time travel
- [ ] memory loss
- [ ] opposite attract
- [ ] student/teacher
- [ ] secret baby
- [ ] May/December
- [ ] accidental pregnancy
- [ ] rich man (chaebol)
- [ ] actor/actress
- [ ] ghosts
- [ ] aliens
- [ ] murder case
- [ ] one night stand
- [ ] thriller
- [ ] Candy/Alpha
- [ ] historical
- [ ] brother's best friend
- [ ] fake relationship
- [ ] bromance
- [ ] childhood friends
- [ ] vampires
- [ ] fantasy
- [ ] workplace

(K-drama Title)

Date Started

Date Completed

Rating
★★★★★

Male Lead (Character Name/Actor Name)

Male Lead (Character Traits)
- ♥
- ♥
- ♥

Female Lead (Character Name/Actress Name)

Female Lead (Character Traits)
- ♥
- ♥
- ♥

Tropes
- [ ] gender switch
- [ ] reverse harem
- [ ] soul switching
- [ ] time travel
- [ ] memory loss
- [ ] opposite attract
- [ ] student/teacher
- [ ] secret baby
- [ ] May/December
- [ ] accidental pregnancy
- [ ] rich man (chaebol)
- [ ] actor/actress
- [ ] ghosts
- [ ] aliens
- [ ] murder case
- [ ] one night stand
- [ ] thriller
- [ ] Candy/Alpha
- [ ] historical
- [ ] brother's best friend
- [ ] fake relationship
- [ ] bromance
- [ ] childhood friends
- [ ] vampires
- [ ] fantasy
- [ ] workplace

_____

(K-drama Title)

Date Started   Date Completed   Rating
⭐⭐⭐⭐⭐

Male Lead (Character Name/Actor Name)

Male Lead (Character Traits)

- ♥
- ♥
- ♥

Female Lead (Character Name/Actress Name)

Female Lead (Character Traits)

- ♥
- ♥
- ♥

Tropes

- [ ] gender switch
- [ ] reverse harem
- [ ] soul switching
- [ ] time travel
- [ ] memory loss
- [ ] opposite attract
- [ ] student/teacher
- [ ] secret baby
- [ ] May/December
- [ ] accidental pregnancy
- [ ] rich man (chaebol)
- [ ] actor/actress
- [ ] ghosts
- [ ] aliens
- [ ] murder case
- [ ] one night stand
- [ ] thriller
- [ ] Candy/Alpha
- [ ] historical
- [ ] brother's best friend
- [ ] fake relationship
- [ ] bromance
- [ ] childhood friends
- [ ] vampires
- [ ] fantasy
- [ ] workplace

_____

(K-drama Title)

Date Started   Date Completed   Rating
⭐⭐⭐⭐⭐

Male Lead (Character Name/Actor Name)

Male Lead (Character Traits)
- ❤
- ❤
- ❤

Female Lead (Character Name/Actress Name)

Female Lead (Character Traits)
- ❤
- ❤
- ❤

Tropes

- [ ] gender switch
- [ ] reverse harem
- [ ] soul switching
- [ ] time travel
- [ ] memory loss
- [ ] opposite attract
- [ ] student/teacher
- [ ] secret baby
- [ ] May/December
- [ ] accidental pregnancy
- [ ] rich man (chaebol)
- [ ] actor/actress
- [ ] ghosts
- [ ] aliens
- [ ] murder case
- [ ] one night stand
- [ ] thriller
- [ ] Candy/Alpha
- [ ] historical
- [ ] brother's best friend
- [ ] fake relationship
- [ ] bromance
- [ ] childhood friends
- [ ] vampires
- [ ] fantasy
- [ ] workplace
- [ ]
- [ ]
- [ ]
- [ ]

2020 KDRAMA MASTER LIST (PART 1)*

*KDramas on Other Lists Not Mentioned Below

- ♥ SO I MARRIED AN ANTI-FAN
- ♥ TOUCH
- ♥ LOVER OF THE PALACE
- ♥ ROMANTIC DOCTOR, TEACHER KIM
- ♥ WINTER VACATION
- ♥ HOW ARE YOU BREAD
- ♥ THE GAME: TOWARDS ZERO
- ♥ SHORT PAPER
- ♥ XX
- ♥ FOREST
- ♥ WHEN THE WEATHER IS FINE
- ♥ REAL:TIME:LOVE 2
- ♥ LIVING WITH A GHOST
- ♥ MY HOLO LOVE
- ♥ ENDING AGAIN
- ♥ JUMP! JUMP! JUMP!
- ♥ the temperature of language: our nineteen
- ♥ something between us, comic book cafe 2
- ♥ BIG PICTURE HOUSE
- ♥ FIGHT HARD, LOVE HARDER (2)
- ♥ FIND ME IN YOUR MEMORY
- ♥ A PIECE OF YOUR MIND
- ♥ MEOW, THE SECRET BOY
- ♥ THE WORLD OF THE MARRIED
- ♥ ECCENTRIC! CHEF MOON

KDRAMA MONTHLY LIST
(month)

Currently Watching

Top Three Favorite Kdramas
- ♥
- ♥
- ♥

K-dramas To Watch
- ♥
- ♥
- ♥
- ♥
- ♥
- ♥
- ♥
- ♥
- ♥

Favorite Oppa (Male Hero)

_____

(K-drama Title)

Date Started   Date Completed   Rating
⭐⭐⭐⭐⭐

Male Lead (Character Name/Actor Name)

Male Lead (Character Traits)

- ♥
- ♥
- ♥

Female Lead (Character Name/Actress Name)

Female Lead (Character Traits)

- ♥
- ♥
- ♥

Tropes

- ☐ gender switch
- ☐ reverse harem
- ☐ soul switching
- ☐ time travel
- ☐ memory loss
- ☐ opposite attract
- ☐ student/teacher
- ☐ secret baby
- ☐ May/December
- ☐ accidental pregnancy
- ☐ rich man (chaebol)
- ☐ actor/actress
- ☐ ghosts
- ☐ aliens
- ☐ murder case
- ☐ one night stand
- ☐ thriller
- ☐ Candy/Alpha
- ☐ historical
- ☐ brother's best friend
- ☐ fake relationship
- ☐ bromance
- ☐ childhood friends
- ☐ vampires
- ☐ fantasy
- ☐ workplace
- ☐
- ☐
- ☐
- ☐

(K-drama Title)

Date Started   Date Completed   Rating
★★★★★

Male Lead (Character Name/Actor Name)

Male Lead (Character Traits)
- ♥
- ♥
- ♥

Female Lead (Character Name/Actress Name)

Female Lead (Character Traits)
- ♥
- ♥
- ♥

Tropes

- [ ] gender switch
- [ ] reverse harem
- [ ] soul switching
- [ ] time travel
- [ ] memory loss
- [ ] opposite attract
- [ ] student/teacher
- [ ] secret baby
- [ ] May/December
- [ ] accidental pregnancy
- [ ] rich man (chaebol)
- [ ] actor/actress
- [ ] ghosts
- [ ] aliens
- [ ] murder case
- [ ] one night stand
- [ ] thriller
- [ ] Candy/Alpha
- [ ] historical
- [ ] brother's best friend
- [ ] fake relationship
- [ ] bromance
- [ ] childhood friends
- [ ] vampires
- [ ] fantasy
- [ ] workplace

(K-drama Title)

Date Started

Date Completed

Rating
★★★★★

Male Lead (Character Name/Actor Name)

Male Lead (Character Traits)

- ♥
- ♥
- ♥

Female Lead (Character Name/Actress Name)

Female Lead (Character Traits)

- ♥
- ♥
- ♥

Tropes

- [ ] gender switch
- [ ] reverse harem
- [ ] soul switching
- [ ] time travel
- [ ] memory loss
- [ ] opposite attract
- [ ] student/teacher
- [ ] secret baby
- [ ] May/December
- [ ] accidental pregnancy
- [ ] rich man (chaebol)
- [ ] actor/actress
- [ ] ghosts
- [ ] aliens
- [ ] murder case
- [ ] one night stand
- [ ] thriller
- [ ] Candy/Alpha
- [ ] historical
- [ ] brother's best friend
- [ ] fake relationship
- [ ] bromance
- [ ] childhood friends
- [ ] vampires
- [ ] fantasy
- [ ] workplace

(K-drama Title)

Date Started

Date Completed

Rating
★★★★★

Male Lead (Character Name/Actor Name)

Male Lead (Character Traits)
- ♥
- ♥
- ♥

Female Lead (Character Name/Actress Name)

Female Lead (Character Traits)
- ♥
- ♥
- ♥

Tropes

☐ gender switch	☐ rich man (chaebol)	☐ fake relationship
☐ reverse harem	☐ actor/actress	☐ bromance
☐ soul switching	☐ ghosts	☐ childhood friends
☐ time travel	☐ aliens	☐ vampires
☐ memory loss	☐ murder case	☐ fantasy
☐ opposite attract	☐ one night stand	☐ workplace
☐ student/teacher	☐ thriller	☐
☐ secret baby	☐ Candy/Alpha	☐
☐ May/December	☐ historical	☐
☐ accidental pregnancy	☐ brother's best friend	☐

_____

(K-drama Title)

Date Started Date Completed Rating
★★★★★

Male Lead (Character Name/Actor Name)

Male Lead (Character Traits)
- ♥
- ♥
- ♥

Female Lead (Character Name/Actress Name)

Female Lead (Character Traits)
- ♥
- ♥
- ♥

Tropes

- [ ] gender switch
- [ ] reverse harem
- [ ] soul switching
- [ ] time travel
- [ ] memory loss
- [ ] opposite attract
- [ ] student/teacher
- [ ] secret baby
- [ ] May/December
- [ ] accidental pregnancy
- [ ] rich man (chaebol)
- [ ] actor/actress
- [ ] ghosts
- [ ] aliens
- [ ] murder case
- [ ] one night stand
- [ ] thriller
- [ ] Candy/Alpha
- [ ] historical
- [ ] brother's best friend
- [ ] fake relationship
- [ ] bromance
- [ ] childhood friends
- [ ] vampires
- [ ] fantasy
- [ ] workplace
- [ ]
- [ ]
- [ ]
- [ ]

_____

(K-drama Title)

Date Started   Date Completed   Rating
★★★★★

Male Lead (Character Name/Actor Name)

Male Lead (Character Traits)

- ♥
- ♥
- ♥

Female Lead (Character Name/Actress Name)

Female Lead (Character Traits)

- ♥
- ♥
- ♥

Tropes

- [ ] gender switch
- [ ] reverse harem
- [ ] soul switching
- [ ] time travel
- [ ] memory loss
- [ ] opposite attract
- [ ] student/teacher
- [ ] secret baby
- [ ] May/December
- [ ] accidental pregnancy
- [ ] rich man (chaebol)
- [ ] actor/actress
- [ ] ghosts
- [ ] aliens
- [ ] murder case
- [ ] one night stand
- [ ] thriller
- [ ] Candy/Alpha
- [ ] historical
- [ ] brother's best friend
- [ ] fake relationship
- [ ] bromance
- [ ] childhood friends
- [ ] vampires
- [ ] fantasy
- [ ] workplace
- [ ]
- [ ]
- [ ]
- [ ]

K-DRAMA
THIS OR THAT
COHABITATION

- [ ] ITS OKAY, THAT'S LOVE

    AGE OF YOUTH [ ]

· · · · · · · · · ·

- [ ] THE LEGEND OF THE BLUE SEA

    FATED TO YOU [ ]

· · · · · · · · · ·

- [ ] I HEAR YOUR VOICE

    OH MY VENUS [ ]

· · · · · · · · · ·

- [ ] OH MY GHOSTESS

    HELLO MONSTER [ ]

· · · · · · · · · ·

- [ ] BECAUSE THIS IS MY FIRST LIFE

    SUSPICIOUS PARTNER [ ]

(month)
KDRAMA MONTHLY LIST

Currently Watching

Top Three Favorite Kdramas
- ♥
- ♥
- ♥

K-dramas To Watch
- ♥
- ♥
- ♥
- ♥
- ♥
- ♥
- ♥
- ♥
- ♥

Favorite Oppa (Male Hero)

(K-drama Title)

Date Started

Date Completed

Rating
★★★★★

Male Lead (Character Name/Actor Name)

Male Lead (Character Traits)
- ♥
- ♥
- ♥

Female Lead (Character Name/Actress Name)

Female Lead (Character Traits)
- ♥
- ♥
- ♥

Tropes

- [ ] gender switch
- [ ] reverse harem
- [ ] soul switching
- [ ] time travel
- [ ] memory loss
- [ ] opposite attract
- [ ] student/teacher
- [ ] secret baby
- [ ] May/December
- [ ] accidental pregnancy
- [ ] rich man (chaebol)
- [ ] actor/actress
- [ ] ghosts
- [ ] aliens
- [ ] murder case
- [ ] one night stand
- [ ] thriller
- [ ] Candy/Alpha
- [ ] historical
- [ ] brother's best friend
- [ ] fake relationship
- [ ] bromance
- [ ] childhood friends
- [ ] vampires
- [ ] fantasy
- [ ] workplace
- [ ]
- [ ]
- [ ]
- [ ]

_____

(K-drama Title)

Date Started   Date Completed   Rating
⭐⭐⭐⭐⭐

Male Lead (Character Name/Actor Name)

Male Lead (Character Traits)
- ♥
- ♥
- ♥

Female Lead (Character Name/Actress Name)

Female Lead (Character Traits)
- ♥
- ♥
- ♥

Tropes

- [ ] gender switch
- [ ] reverse harem
- [ ] soul switching
- [ ] time travel
- [ ] memory loss
- [ ] opposite attract
- [ ] student/teacher
- [ ] secret baby
- [ ] May/December
- [ ] accidental pregnancy
- [ ] rich man (chaebol)
- [ ] actor/actress
- [ ] ghosts
- [ ] aliens
- [ ] murder case
- [ ] one night stand
- [ ] thriller
- [ ] Candy/Alpha
- [ ] historical
- [ ] brother's best friend
- [ ] fake relationship
- [ ] bromance
- [ ] childhood friends
- [ ] vampires
- [ ] fantasy
- [ ] workplace
- [ ]
- [ ]
- [ ]
- [ ]

_____

(K-drama Title)

Date Started   Date Completed   Rating
⭐⭐⭐⭐⭐

Male Lead (Character Name/Actor Name)

Male Lead (Character Traits)

- ♥
- ♥
- ♥

Female Lead (Character Name/Actress Name)

Female Lead (Character Traits)

- ♥
- ♥
- ♥

Tropes

- [ ] gender switch
- [ ] reverse harem
- [ ] soul switching
- [ ] time travel
- [ ] memory loss
- [ ] opposite attract
- [ ] student/teacher
- [ ] secret baby
- [ ] May/December
- [ ] accidental pregnancy
- [ ] rich man (chaebol)
- [ ] actor/actress
- [ ] ghosts
- [ ] aliens
- [ ] murder case
- [ ] one night stand
- [ ] thriller
- [ ] Candy/Alpha
- [ ] historical
- [ ] brother's best friend
- [ ] fake relationship
- [ ] bromance
- [ ] childhood friends
- [ ] vampires
- [ ] fantasy
- [ ] workplace

(K-drama Title)

Date Started

Date Completed

Rating
★★★★★

Male Lead (Character Name/Actor Name)

Male Lead (Character Traits)
- ♥
- ♥
- ♥

Female Lead (Character Name/Actress Name)

Female Lead (Character Traits)
- ♥
- ♥
- ♥

Tropes

- [ ] gender switch
- [ ] reverse harem
- [ ] soul switching
- [ ] time travel
- [ ] memory loss
- [ ] opposite attract
- [ ] student/teacher
- [ ] secret baby
- [ ] May/December
- [ ] accidental pregnancy
- [ ] rich man (chaebol)
- [ ] actor/actress
- [ ] ghosts
- [ ] aliens
- [ ] murder case
- [ ] one night stand
- [ ] thriller
- [ ] Candy/Alpha
- [ ] historical
- [ ] brother's best friend
- [ ] fake relationship
- [ ] bromance
- [ ] childhood friends
- [ ] vampires
- [ ] fantasy
- [ ] workplace

(K-drama Title)

Date Started

Date Completed

Rating
★★★★★

Male Lead (Character Name/Actor Name)

Male Lead (Character Traits)
- ♥
- ♥
- ♥

Female Lead (Character Name/Actress Name)

Female Lead (Character Traits)
- ♥
- ♥
- ♥

Tropes

- [ ] gender switch
- [ ] reverse harem
- [ ] soul switching
- [ ] time travel
- [ ] memory loss
- [ ] opposite attract
- [ ] student/teacher
- [ ] secret baby
- [ ] May/December
- [ ] accidental pregnancy
- [ ] rich man (chaebol)
- [ ] actor/actress
- [ ] ghosts
- [ ] aliens
- [ ] murder case
- [ ] one night stand
- [ ] thriller
- [ ] Candy/Alpha
- [ ] historical
- [ ] brother's best friend
- [ ] fake relationship
- [ ] bromance
- [ ] childhood friends
- [ ] vampires
- [ ] fantasy
- [ ] workplace
- [ ]
- [ ]
- [ ]
- [ ]

(K-drama Title)

Date Started

Date Completed

Rating
★★★★★

Male Lead (Character Name/Actor Name)

Male Lead (Character Traits)
- ♥
- ♥
- ♥

Female Lead (Character Name/Actress Name)

Female Lead (Character Traits)
- ♥
- ♥
- ♥

Tropes

- [ ] gender switch
- [ ] reverse harem
- [ ] soul switching
- [ ] time travel
- [ ] memory loss
- [ ] opposite attract
- [ ] student/teacher
- [ ] secret baby
- [ ] May/December
- [ ] accidental pregnancy
- [ ] rich man (chaebol)
- [ ] actor/actress
- [ ] ghosts
- [ ] aliens
- [ ] murder case
- [ ] one night stand
- [ ] thriller
- [ ] Candy/Alpha
- [ ] historical
- [ ] brother's best friend
- [ ] fake relationship
- [ ] bromance
- [ ] childhood friends
- [ ] vampires
- [ ] fantasy
- [ ] workplace

2020 KDRAMA MASTER LIST (PART 1)*
*KDramas on Other Lists Not Mentioned Below

- ♥ ONCE AGAIN
- ♥ ROMANCE TALKING
- ♥ SOMEHOW FAMILY
- ♥ FATAL PROMISE
- ♥ BEST MISTAKE SEASON 2
- ♥ HOW TO BUY A FRIEND
- ♥ ORDINARY BUT SPECIAL
- ♥ BORN AGAIN
- ♥ BRILLIANT HERITAGE
- ♥ THE WORLD OF MY 17
- ♥ EXCITING TO WORK
- ♥ MERMAID PRINCE
- ♥ WHEN MY LOVE BLOOMS
- ♥ CAST: THE GOLDEN AGE OF INSIDERS
- ♥ FIX YOU
- ♥ LIE OF A LIE

www.ingramcontent.com/pod-product-compliance
Lightning Source LLC
Chambersburg PA
CBHW052114110526
44592CB00013B/1605

9 781947 131071